Acknowledgement

I gratefully acknowledge the help given to me by myself in the compilation and editing of those phoenix. Me has always been a source of inspiration to me .

With my mature and practical assistance helped me in bringing out this selection of enlightenments from various saying by my anonymous Mentors.That I took them as my life lessons

Saurabh Bhatnagar

Preface

Theses selection contains many Phrases that are "life lessons".

Which i unite from my day to day routine from My past and reflected to them from time to time again and again and derive great inspiration strength and solace. My efforts will thus not be fruitful and rewarding but the process is in between is encouraging. In my whole life i traveled from many phases of my life and God has be kind in my all endeavors.

When i was 22 years My parents were died very early. i along with my younger brother and relatives. We were able to pick up the pieces and to build a very precise bonding. In my early years i had not enough time for reading and writing so i gathered the lessons and the sublesson in my diary about two decade back i was expected that i have to collect and resemble them for the world. Very softly i present this collection to the different World of people and help all the people.

"Miscellaneous for all Souls"

"Journey Begins"

S.no.   Content.   Page Number.

1.   One Liner Inspirations

2.   Multi Liner Inspiration

3.   Miscellaneous Insipriation

❖ The high destiny of an individual is to rule rather than serve. Mr. Einstein

★ When the ship is sinking only Water can save it.

★ Self discipline is the way to achieve.

★ Where the one goes energy flows.

★ When I am with me nothing seems to matter.

★ When I need to cry me lends me Shoulder.

★ It's a sin to be unhappy in such a beautiful way.

★ Me is dependable on me.

★ When I listen to me me knows me.

★ When I am around everything is fun.

★ Me and I together make magic and miracles.

★ I and Me both can't do without each other.

★ Me a perfect matches is with me.

★ Me taught me the meaning of love and sharing.

★ Me Thinking of me and a wonderful Touch of Love to my life.

★ Me understand me when me is sobbing.

★ Every moment spent with me is one filled with fun.

★ Me love me give me that is best for me.

★ One dreaming of success one must wake up and be punctual to fulfil it.

★ Nature is Music for the soul.

★ I am a special person I was created with love.

★ I do not need to look like or act like anyone else.

★ I love everything about me because god give me as it is.

★ God loves me like just the way I am.

★ I love who I am, I am enough I will not let other people makes me feel bad about myself.

❖ Lead kindly The light from the Unreal to the real from darkness to the light from death to immortality. Jivamukti Yoga

★ See we will survive even when the whole world leaves us alone.

★ Chirping moments distant windows light twinkling and glow becking warm through this wintery show.

❖ We must accept finite disappointment but we must never lose infinite hope. Sir Martin Luther King Jr.

★ Self discipline is the way to achieve.

★ Something is everything about me .

★ Nature please feel free to enlight me.

★ Me moving into the darkness to find me.

❖ Be water my friend.

★ I shut my "I"s to open my eyes.

★ Be stillness revealed the secret of eternity. The more you pay attention the weirder it becomes.

❖ I am not impressed by money status or job title i am

impressed by the way you treat other human beings.

❖ Enlightenment has No believe no gender no sexuality no race no age no mentality you are consciousness.

★ Whatever you hear about me please believe it I no longer have time to explain myself you can also add some if you want.

❖ Go find yourself so you can find me. Rumi

★ Protector of light knows whats in his heart.

- ❖ I am 99% sure you don't like me but I am 100% sure I don't care.

- ❖ Dear problems, please give me some discount afterall, I am your regular customer.

- ★ I feel lost Inside myself and be inspired but don't copy. My dear heart, don't fail me now.

- ❖ I am too insane to explain and you are too much normal to understand.

- ★ You did not born here to obey your fictitious Dreams, you came here to bring heaven to earth.

- ❖ Don't shy away from 4 things: old clothes, old friends, old mum and dad and simply living.

- ❖ A life spent making mistakes is not only more honorable but more useful than a life spent doing nothing.

- ❖ Sometimes God breaks your heart to save your soul.

- ★ I asked god what is poison, Excess.

- ❖ In the end we all become stories.

- ★ Ignorance is used by the by the strong.

- ★ In all darkness there is light and all night there is darkness.

- ★ One never exists in and that's best quality.

- ★ Gnosis the mystical science of inner knowing.

- ★ It's about progress not perfection.

- ★ So mother says you only live once.

★ I am realitition ask me about reality.

❖ Warriors are not the one who always win but the ones that always fight.

❖ Being both soft and strong is a combination very few have mastered.

★ Do you know the distance between your mouth and Your Ears how you speak to yourself you are listening.

★ Take care how you think about yourself because you are becoming.

❖ No excuses no explanation you don't win on emotion you win on execution.

★ I am in competition with no one.

❖ I have no desire to play the games of being better than anyone i am simply trying to be better than the person I was yesterday.

❖ You need power only when you want to do something harmful otherwise love is enough to get everything done. Mr Chapplin

★ The best apology is changed behavior.

❖ There is a message in the way a person Treats you just listen.

❖ The one is always free and is always alone the mind is only dreaming "Papa ji".

❖ Never judge people by their past People learn, people change, people move on.

❖ Work while they sleep, learn while they party, save while they spend, then live like they dream.

❖ I am a travellor of both space and time.

★ Love your fear and they will dissolve.

❖ You did not lose your mind trying to understand mine.

❖ Even though you want to run even when it's heavy and difficult even though you are not quite sure of the way through.

★ The sound of your existence might be too loud for some instead of turning down your volume align *with those who alike the music aloud.*

★ *Healing happens by feeling.*

★ *One is nowhere between mind and finding soul.*

★ *Father once said with certainty that I am both its origin and The dissolution.*

❖ *The secret of change is to focus all your energy not on fighting the old but on building the new.*

❖ *A wise man can learn more from foolish questions than a*

fool can learn from wiser answer.

❖ I am gonna make rest of my life the best of my life.

❖ You must master new way of Thinking before you master a new way of living.

❖ He who blames others has a long way to go on his journey; he who believes himself is a Halfway there is who blame no one has arrived.

❖ *One is more powerful than you know and they fear the day you discover it.*

★ *Mass and energy are different things.*

❖ *I fear not the man who has practiced 10,000 kicks once but I fear the man who practiced one kick 10,000 Times.*

❖ *Disciples and devotees are the most of them worshiping the teapot instead of drinking the tea.*

❖ When you are born in the world you don't fit and it's because you were born to help create a new one.

❖ Your mind will always believe everything you tell it feels the feed of hope feels the feed of truth feels the feed of love.

❖ Never apologize for being too passionate, it's too strange, too curious because you are not a normal individual and it's a blessing.

❖ If the news is fake, imagine how bad the history.....is ?

❖ Do the better you know until it becomes good when it becomes good do the best.

★ The act of spreading knowledge is one of the highest expressions of unconditional love that one can ever give.

★ Space and time are very different things where space is relative and time is absolute.

★ Gravity is force, gravity is a geometry.

★ Science without religion is lame religion without science is blind Mr.Einstein

❖ I meditate, I burn, I create candles, I drink green tea and I still want to Smack some people.

★ Suddenly a sort of flash comes out of me like something electric. It jumps out and touches the person who has made me cross.

❖ My favorite thing in the world is a quiz show University

challenge so you can see what kind of sad person I am.

❖ One beautiful heart is better than a thousand beautiful faces.

★ I made a mistake and hurt myself.

★ Practice your mind to calm in every situation.

❖ Reading can seriously damage my ignorance.

★ Once upon a time I lost my smile.

❖ There is always a difference between knowing the path and walking it.

★ The hardest thing for people to see is themselves.

★ I thought I don't have much in common with all the people.

★ To be handsome means to be yourself you don't need to be accepted by others, you just need to accept yourself.

❖ The most beautiful music in the world is our own Heartbeat.

❖ Don't let negative and toxic people rent space in your head

Raise your rent and kick their ass out.

❖ I have been fighting since I was a child. I am not a survivor, I am a warrior.

❖ When you really pay attention everything is your Guru.

★ Cat crossing people's path means an animal going to the toilet.

★ I looked up there and I did not find God he or she lives within.

★ There are always goodbyes because we die and transform to see forever in the next Dimension where souls are free.

★ In the strongest direction one must walk alone.

★ Just be silent and patient when you are hurt by the words their words will echo in their mind .

★ Introspection is the conversation with the universe Saurabh.

★ I am different human and it just not ok it's fucking awesome.

❖ The heart is not jealous of my parents. I will never have a kid as cool as theirs....!

★ I have been fighting since I was a child I am not a survivor I am a caretaker.

★ Symbolism is the language of God.

❖ Lessons in life will be repeated until they are learnt.

❖ If I am wrong, educate me please don't belittle me.

★ You are innocent.

❖ How people treat me is their karma, how I respond is mine.

★ As soon as I love myself.

❖ When I was born I was given a name, a religion, a nationality and identity and I spent my life defending it.

★ I Don't adjust my thinking because I can't.

❖ I don't fix problems, I solve my thinking then problems fix themselves.

❖ The only way to defeat a toxic person is to not play.

★ Every change brings you lesson you are not ready for but you need to accept it.

❖ *If Idiots could fly, this Place must be an airport.*

❖ *Dear heart please don't get involved in every situation. Your job is to pump blood thats it.*

❖ *I don't make mistakes I date them*

★ *Oh God I love you.*

★ *Open your pineal gland to the ancestor and you will understand the language of spirits.*

❖ *Don't try so hard to adjust and after all I am not here to stay.*

★ The one who opens your heart is me.

★ The one who penned me is me.

★ Kindness make me the beautiful person in the world no matter how I look like.

❖ Guided by the spirit not by the egos.

❖ I love my six pack so much that I protect it from a layer of fat.

❖ Love me great hate me even better think I am ugly don't look at me Don't know me don't judge me think you know me you have no idea.

★ I like to be alone so much.

★ If I am tired I learnt to rest not to quit.

★ Listen, patients are going to die.

❖ Hear to the wind it talks, listen to the silence it speaks, feels to your heart it knows.

❖ Not the waking language but the one sharing the same feeling understand each others.

❖ Your life is your message to the world please be sure its inspiring.

★ My energy speaks before I find words.

★ Simple life happy life.

★ I cannot teach anybody anything I just make them think.

★ Today I will learn how to sleep.

★ I killed myself by loving someone in very earlier days.

❖ I don't vibe with many but if i do it's from the depth of my heart.

★ Remember the high vibrational being within and found light and energy in human body that i temporarily occupy.

❖ The person who says it can't be done should not interrupt the person doing it.

❖ Your energy speaks to you before you even speak.

★ If you die before you die then you won't die when you die

❖ Be proud of yourself for how hard you are trying.

★ No stop following people because they are lost.

★ I am letters, words, phrases and finally the spell.

❖ Distance doesn't separate people, it's silence.

❖ Silence is not heard as its full of answers.

❖ I may not mention me on facebook post but i always mention me in my prayers and i thought its way better.

★ Forgiving me is my gift to me moving on is my gift to myself.

❖ For success in life you need two things: ignorance and confidence.

❖ At any moment you gather up your courage and chose to heal then you will know the truth and the truth will set you free.

❖ In the end all i learned was how to be strong alone.

❖ Breath deeply to bring your mind to your body.

❖ Some people awaken spiritually with the help of meditation and introspection.

❖ Knowing knowledge and wisdom is a powerful weapon and arm yours with it.

- ❖ I have some more whispering conversations in my head than i do in real life.

- ❖ Life lesson i learnt no one sees how much you do for them what they only see what you don't do.

- ❖ One true son can teach that all mens are not the same.

- ❖ Before you share your secrets make sure that your listener is not a speaker in definitely not a script writer

- ❖ Come and taste the rainbow.

❖ Don't let others make you forget that.

★ Your life is a series of lessons in becoming yourself.

❖ Although I am a lonely person in my daily life, my awareness of belonging.

❖ To the invisible community of those who strive for truth, beauty and justices that has prevented me from feeling of isolation.

★ My biggest Mistake is that I lied to my parents for someone who always lied to me.

- ❖ I can't fix stupid but I can't watch them in action on Facebook everyday.

- ★ May your God treat you well.

- ❖ The only true wisdom is in knowing you know nothing.

- ❖ A good book makes you want to live in the story.

- ❖ Great books give you no choices.

- ❖ The ability to observe without judgment is the highest form of intelligence.

- ❖ I don't need to know you, I can feel your energy and it's living inside of my heart.

- ❖ I am not from the earth, I am just a passenger.

- ❖ I grow when problems are not easy i grow when i solve them.

- ★ Now I am no longer forcing things, what flows flows, what destroys, I only have space and energy for the things that are meant for me.

- ★ Hate is heavy and I let it go.

- ❖ I may look innocent but i screenshot a lot.

- ❖ Don't panic, organize one day and the reality will be better than you dream.

- ★ Water is life for the galaxy its everywhere and give life to more planets and preserve it in its form.

- ★ I absolutely refuse to waste my magic on anyone who can't see how rare I am to stop trying to recycle what god is trying to replace.

- ★ According to science people who are punctual are probably more creative.

❖ I always love when someone remembers something i told them a long time ago.

❖ I either keep it all inside or say exactly how i feel with no filters there is no in between.

★ I either love or leave.

★ Choose people who choose you.

★ What is love love is the absence of judgements.

❖ What if plants and animals are actually farming us giving us food and oxygen until we die then they eat us as manure

.

★ Three things: pen paper thoughts.

❖ Mankind was born on earth; it was never meant to die here.

❖ My strongest muscle and worst enemy is my mind and I trained it well.

❖ The world is full of monsters with friendly faces and angels full of scars.

❖ Don't study me, you won't graduate.

❖ Sometimes it's just better to just remain silent and smile.

❖ What you heard try asking me first.

❖ I am you, you are me, we are one.

❖ Planet earth is not my home, I am just passing through.

❖ There is not birth and death but arrival and departure from one form to another.

❖ Eyes opened, head raised, spirit elevated, feeling guided, ego humble.

❖ Don't treat people as bad as they are, treat them as good as you are.

★ Me & me have this array.

★ Me and I have this arrangement if he wakes me up to see another day I promise to try to be a better person than I was yesterday.

❖ Be crazy be stupid , be silly, be weird , be whatever because life is too short to be anything but happy.

❖ Don't ask me why I am silent because if I speak I will speak only about space time, time travel black holes, quantum entanglement etc and then everyone else remains silent.

❖ Definition of stupid knowing the truth seeing the truth but still believing in lies.

❖ Honesty has a power that very few can handle.

❖ I might as well call you google because you have everything that i am looking for.

❖ Where focus goes energy flows.

❖ Sometimes we need fantasy to survive reality.

❖ I don't want to be your second choice.

❖ 7 trillions smiles but yours is my favorite.

❖ I crave love so deep that the ocean would be jealous.

★ Do not say I will pay you back for this wrong, leave it for the lord and he will deliver it to the right time.

❖ I hate small talk i want talk about atoms, death aliens sex magic, intelligence intellect, the meaning of life in faraway galaxy and more galaxies.

❖ May if we tell people the brain is an app they will start using it.

❖ Knowing others is intelligence, knowing yourself is true wisdom, mastering others is strength, mastering others is good, mastering yourself is true power.

❖ If you realize that you have enough you are truly rich.

★ You are my end and my beginning even i win i am losing.

❖ Give yourself permission to shine, you were made to live a big life not hide in the shadows.

❖ A book in my hand and nature beside me.

❖ One reality is better than your dreams.

❖ Your face with marked with lines of life put there by love and laughter, suffering and tears its beautiful.

- ❖ No man ever steps in the same river twice for its not the same river and he is not the same man.

- ❖ Don't fear death, fear the unlived life in nature.

- ❖ Me trying to explain to toxic people why I can't be around them.

- I understand myself only after I destroyed myself and only in the process of fixing myself did i know who i really was.

- ❖ You are the thief of the your joy.

- ❖ There is no birth or death but arrival and departure from one form to another.

- ❖ Football doesn't build character, it eliminates the weak one.

- ❖ What are you twelve oh yes on a scale of one to ten.

- ❖ I am actually not funny i am just really mean and people think i am joking.

- ❖ I hate how chocolates immediately melt on my fingers. I mean, am i that hot.

- ❖ If people are trying to bring you down it means you are above them.

- ❖ We always work for tomorrow but when tomorrow comes instead off enjoying it we again think of a better today.

- ❖ A man with dreams needs a woman with vision.

- ❖ This little light of nine i am going to let it shine.

- ❖ Blessed thankful and focused.

❖ Laughter is the medicine but if you are laughing with no reason you need medicine.

❖ I was in my kitchen cleaning when suddenly i realized o.m.g i am late for facebook.

❖ I used to be a people person but people ruined that for me.

❖ Some people are like clouds one day they are gone its just a beautiful day.

❖ Even the nicest people have their limits.

❖ With great power comes great electric bills.

- ❖ Hey i will be back in 5 minutes just read the message again.

- ❖ Dear karma, I have a list of people you missed.

- ❖ There are two ways to argue with the woman neither works because we are one 10=10.

- ❖ Making mistake is better then faking perfection.

- ❖ Life is short, time is fast no reply no rewind so enjoy every moment as it comes.

❖ You are my end and my beginning.

❖ You could not handle me even if i came with instructions.

❖ I Live I Die I Live again. I am from the Sun just witness me.

❖ Your body is 72% water and I am thirsty.

❖ Logic will get you from A to B emotion will take you everywhere.

❖ I am only responsible for what i say, i say not for what you understand.

❖ I think thinking is not illegal yet.

❖ One lie is enough to question all the truth.

❖ I don't hate you i just lost respect for you.

❖ I heard before that you are player nice to meet you i am the coach.

❖ Always approach a bull from the front a horse from the behind and they kick your ass out of your mouth.

❖ Never approach a bull from the front a horse from the

behind an idiot, fool, liar from any direction.

❖ Yours tribe attracts your tribe.

❖ Everything happens for a reason, crazy and proud of it.

❖ I hope karma will slap you in face before i do.

❖ Why life keep teaching me lessons i have no desire to learn sometimes.

❖ If plan "A" doesn't work the dictionary of alphabets has 25 more letters stay cool.

- ❖ No intelligent species would destroy their planet.

- ❖ Love vs like pluck a flower or water it daily .

- ❖ The who understand it understand life buddha.

- ❖ Once you believe signs are every where.

- ❖ You can't force a connection we meet the right people at the right time under right circumstances through natural vibration.

- ❖ A man is complete until he has married then he is completely finished.

- ❖ Don't be afraid to change. You may lose something good but you may gain something better.

- ❖ One mistake and very one judges you.

- ❖ It is better to be hated for what you are than to be loved for what you are not learn from everyone and follow no one.

- ❖ A wise man fills his brain before emptying his mouth.

- ❖ Recognise the divine power within be your own guiding light elevate yourself with consistent efforts practice and self discipline 2G.

- ❖ Be someone light when they are hopeless.

- ❖ People laugh because I am different i laugh because they are all the same.

❖ People tell i have a bad attitude just because i speak what they keep thinking.

❖ Be the hero of your own life story.

❖ For all those men who think a woman's place is in the kitchen remember that where the knives are kept.

❖ But with the presence of mind.

Thank you

Saurabh Bhatnagar

www.ingramcontent.com/pod-product-compliance
Lightning Source LLC
LaVergne TN
LVHW061622070526
838199LV00078B/7382